THE WHEELS
The Friendship Race

LE RUOTE
La gara dell'amicizia

Inna Nusinsky
Illustrations by Michael Jay Roque

www.kidkiddos.com
Copyright©2015 by S.A.Publishing ©2017 by KidKiddos Books Ltd.
support@kidkiddos.com

All rights reserved. No part of this book may be reproduced in any form or by any electronic or mechanical means, including information storage and retrieval systems, without written permission from the publisher or author, except in the case of a reviewer, who may quote brief passages embodied in critical articles or in a review.

Tutti i diritti sono riservati. Nessuna parte di questa pubblicazione può essere riprodotta, memorizzata in sistemi di recupero o trasmessa in qualsiasi forma o attraverso qualsiasi mezzo elettronico, meccanico, mediante fotocopiatura, registrazione o altro, senza l'autorizzazione del possessore del copyright.
Second edition, 2019

Translated from English by Sara Adinolfi
Traduzione dall'inglese di Sara Adinolfi

Library and Archives Canada Cataloguing in Publication
The Wheels: The Friendship race (Italian Bilingual Edition)
ISBN: 978-1-5259-1623-6 paperback
ISBN: 978-1-77268-887-0 hardcover
ISBN: 978-1-77268-885-6 eBook

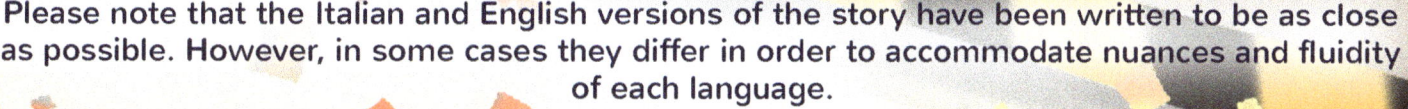

Please note that the Italian and English versions of the story have been written to be as close as possible. However, in some cases they differ in order to accommodate nuances and fluidity of each language.

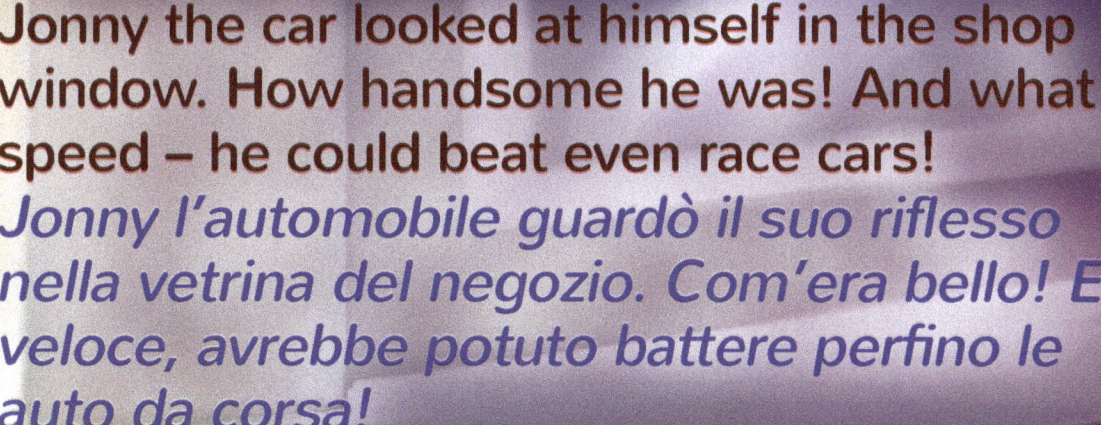

Jonny the car looked at himself in the shop window. How handsome he was! And what speed – he could beat even race cars!
Jonny l'automobile guardò il suo riflesso nella vetrina del negozio. Com'era bello! E veloce, avrebbe potuto battere perfino le auto da corsa!

"I'm the pride of the neighborhood," he yelled.
"Sono l'orgoglio del quartiere," gridò.

Just then, two braking sounds broke his daydream.
Mentre sognava a occhi aperti fu interrotto dal suono di due frenate.

He saw them reflected in the glass window – his friends Mike the bike and Scott the scooter.
Subito vide nel vetro le immagini dei suoi amici Mike la bici e Scott il monopattino.

"Hey Jonny!" they said. "What's up?"
"Ciao Jonny!" dissero gli amici. "Che succede?"

"Feeling like a little race today," said Jonny, puffing his tires. "But there's no one I can race with."

"Ho voglia di correre un po' oggi," rispose Jonny, sgonfiando le gomme. "Ma non c'è nessuno con cui posso farlo."

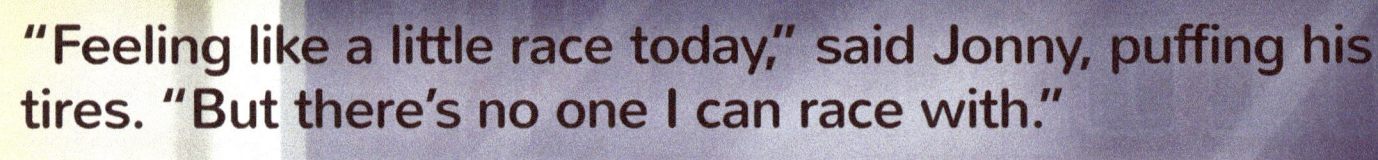

"We can race with you!" exclaimed Mike.
"Possiamo correre noi con te!" esclamò Mike.

"That's what friends are for!" added Scott.
"È a questo che servono gli amici!" aggiunse Scott.

Jonny didn't show much enthusiasm. "Mmm... A champion needs an equal to compete with."
Jonny non mostrò molto entusiasmo. "Mmm...un campione deve gareggiare con un suo simile."

Mike and Scott looked at each other. A cloud passed over their faces.
Mike e Scott si scambiarono uno sguardo. I loro volti si rabbuiarono.

"Are we not good?" asked Mike.
"Non siamo all'altezza?" chiese Mike.

"Oh, you're good," Jonny made a face in the glass window. "But not good enough."
"Certo che lo siete," Jonny si guardò ancora nella vetrina. "Ma non abbastanza."

"Okay, Jonny," said Scott. "We challenge you to a race right now! Let's do Hill Road and see who finishes first."

"Va bene Jonny, " disse Scott. "Ti sfidiamo, facciamo una gara adesso! Facciamo tutta la Hill Road e vediamo chi arriva prima."

Jonny considered it with a smirk.

Jonny fece un sorrisetto.

As they reached Hill Road, the race began.
Giunti ai piedi di Hill Road la corsa ebbe inizio.

It started with a steep climb. Jonny roared and in seconds was over the incline.
C'era una salita ripida. Si sentì il rombo di Jonny che in un attimo fu in cima al pendio.

Mike the bike was already half way... But poor Scott the scooter was huffing and puffing, slowly climbing up.
Mike la bici era a metà percorso...ma il povero Scott il monopattino era senza fiato, e riuscì a salire a fatica.

Jonny reached the hill and stopped. He looked at the rearview mirror – his friends were far behind.
Jonny raggiunse l'altura e si fermò. Guardò negli specchietti retrovisori, i suoi amici erano ancora lontani.

He was bored. At least the music on the radio was good! He closed his eyes and started moving to the beat.

Si annoiava. Almeno la musica alla radio era di suo gusto! Chiuse gli occhi e iniziò a muoversi a ritmo.

Suddenly, something whirred past him and he jolted his eyes open. There was only smoke. Mike?
All'improvviso un ronzìo gli passò di fianco. C'era soltanto polvere. Mike?

Before he could say a word something else went by. Jonny looked through the disappearing smoke—that was Scott racing ahead!

Prima che potesse aprire bocca, qualcos'altro lo superò. Jonny guardò nella polvere che si dissolveva, e vide Scott correre davanti a lui!

No way! Now he panicked. He should win!

Non è possibile! Fu preso dal panico. Doveva vincere lui!

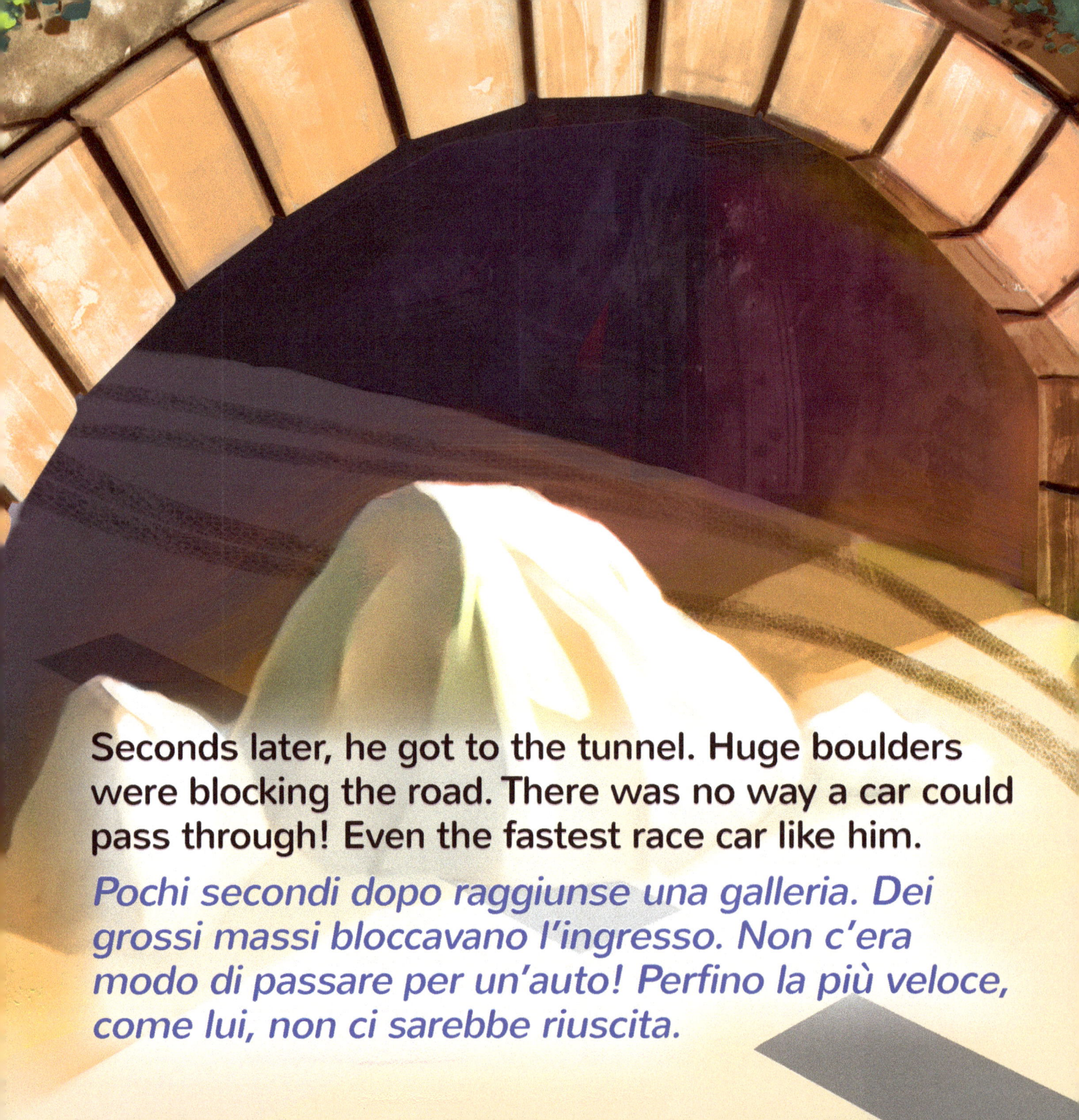

Seconds later, he got to the tunnel. Huge boulders were blocking the road. There was no way a car could pass through! Even the fastest race car like him.

Pochi secondi dopo raggiunse una galleria. Dei grossi massi bloccavano l'ingresso. Non c'era modo di passare per un'auto! Perfino la più veloce, come lui, non ci sarebbe riuscita.

But then, he saw the tire marks of both Mike and Scott. They had negotiated their way around the stone boulders! Jonny sighed.

Poi vide i segni delle ruote sia di Mike che di Scott. Erano riusciti a girare intorno ai massi e passare! Jonny sospirò.

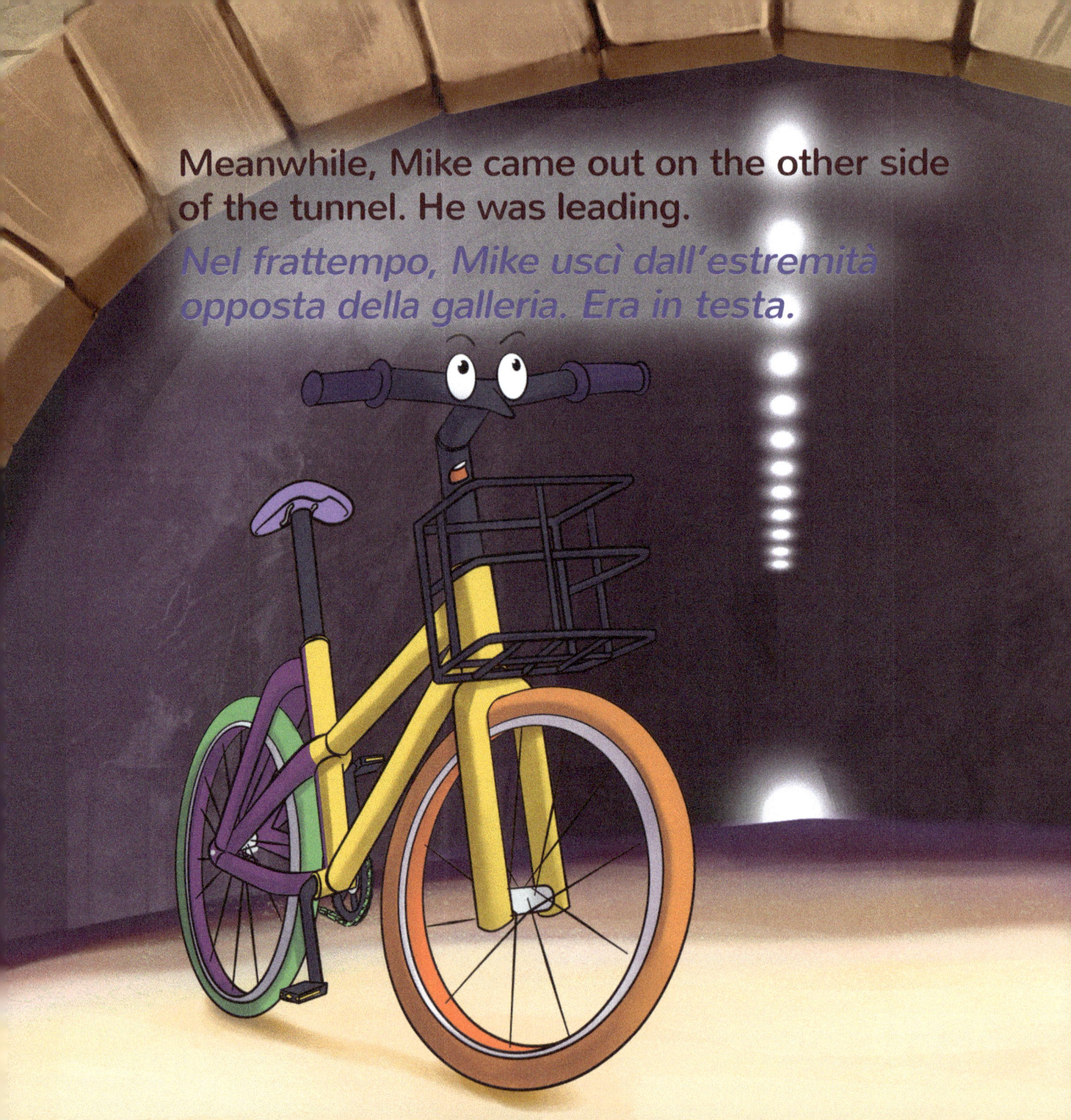

Meanwhile, Mike came out on the other side of the tunnel. He was leading.

Nel frattempo, Mike uscì dall'estremità opposta della galleria. Era in testa.

What kind of a win is that when your friends lose? he thought.
Che razza di vittoria è, se a perdere è un tuo amico? Pensò.

In seconds, Scott was next to him.
Subito dopo Scott apparve al suo fianco.

"Why did you stop, Mike?" he asked. "You could've won the race!"
"Perché ti sei fermato, Mike?" gli chiese. "Avresti potuto vincere la gara!"

"Yeah but...Jonny could be stuck back there..." said Mike, looking towards the tunnel.
"Si ma...Jonny potrebbe essere rimasto bloccato laggiù..." disse Mike, guardando attraverso la galleria.

A moment of silence passed by.
Ci fu un momento di silenzio.

"Shall we go to check up him?" Scott asked.
"Potremmo andare a controllare?" chiese Scott.

A smile formed on Mike's face. "Let's go!" he yelled and turned back.
Sul volto di Mike apparve un sorriso. "Andiamo!" disse, e si voltò.

At the blocked tunnel, Jonny was sad. Not because he was losing the race but because he was lonely.

Davanti al passaggio bloccato Jonny era triste. Non perché stava perdendo la gara, ma perché era solo.

Suddenly he heard a sound of wheels. Those were Scott and Mike!

Poi, all'improvviso, udì un rumore di ruote. Quelli erano Scott e Mike!

"Mike, Let's move these boulders so Jonny can pass," said Scott.

"Mike, spostiamo questi massi, così anche Jonny potrà passare!" lo incitò Scott.

The friends started to work together, pushing the rocks out of the way.

I due amici iniziarono a lavorare insieme, liberando il passaggio dalle rocce.

It wasn't easy, but they nudged and nudged and soon there was enough space for Jonny to squeeze through.

Non fu facile, ma, spinta dopo spinta, ci fu abbastanza spazio per far passare Jonny.

Giggling, they reached the end of Hill Road.
Ridendo, raggiunsero la fine di Hill Road.

"We've won the race—all of us!" exclaimed Mike and Scott.

"Abbiamo vinto tutti e tre!" esclamarono Mike e Scott.

Only Jonny was quiet. "I behaved badly with you," he admitted. "I realized it late, guys that together we can do much more. Thank you, my friends, for helping me understand that!"

Soltanto Jonny era un po' triste. "Mi sono comportato male con voi," ammise. "L'ho capito dopo che insieme possiamo fare molto di più. Grazie amici miei per avermelo fatto capire!"

Suddenly, there was applause, cheering for this wonderful bunch of three terrific friends...

Poi un applauso accolse questa splendido trio di amici...

Friends who discovered that none of them was as good as all of them.

Amici che hanno capito di essere migliori quando sono insieme.

www.ingramcontent.com/pod-product-compliance
Lightning Source LLC
Chambersburg PA
CBHW061146070526
44584CB00033B/4431